CHOICES

DARE TO BE DIFFERENT

AUTHOR
Lyman Coleman

PROJECT ENGINEER
Matthew Lockhart

CONTRIBUTORS
Jeff Coleman, Richard Guy

TYPESETTING
Sharon Penington

COVER DESIGN
Erika Tiepel

Photo on cover and repeated throughout book:
©1994, Robert Torrez/Tony Stone Images'

Scripture taken from
Today's English Version
Second Edition © 1992
Old Testament:
© American Bible Society 1976, 1992
New Testament :
© American Bible Society 1966, 1971, 1976, 1992
Published by
Thomas Nelson Publishers
Used by permission.

Seven Sessions on Morality

Session	Bible Story	Team Building Goal
1 HOLY GRAIL	Pearl of Great Price/Matthew 13:44-46	Team Sign-Up
2 POSSESSIONS	Rich Fool/Luke 12:13-21	Learning to Share
3 USING YOUR ABILITIES	Talents/Matthew 25:14-30	Going Deeper
4 CONCERNS / CAUSES	Salt & Light/Matthew 5:13-16	Affirmation
5 SEX	Potiphar's Wife/Genesis 39:1-20	Getting Personal
6 SPIRITUAL CALLING	Peter's Call/Luke 5:1-11	Learning to Care
7 BOTTOM LINE	House Builders/Matthew 7:24-27	Team Celebration

SERENDIPITY HOUSE / Box 1012 / Littleton, CO 80160 / TOLL FREE 1-800-525-9563

© 1994 Serendipity House. All Rights Reserved.

95 96 97 98 99 /CH/ 6 5 4

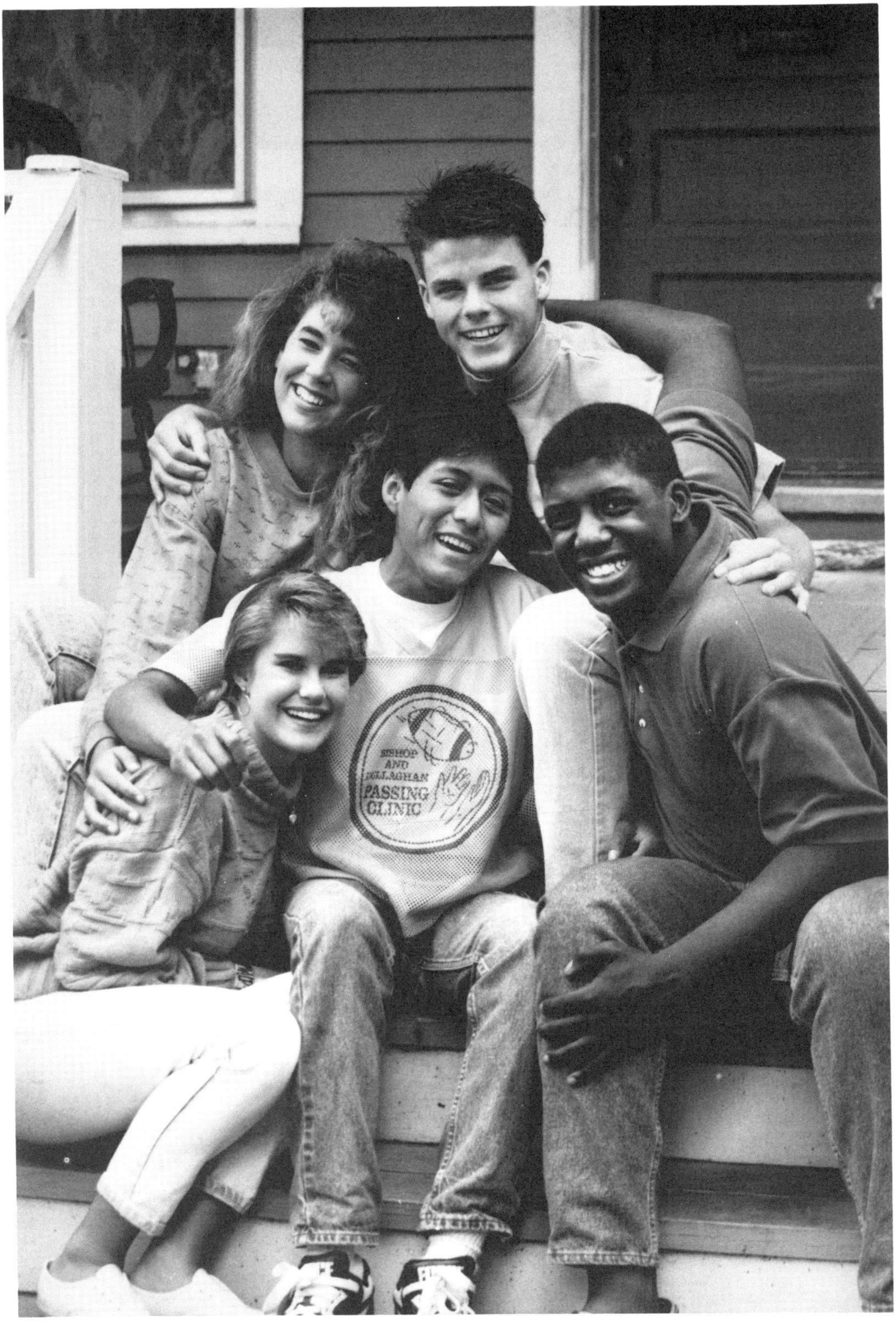
AND
PASSING
CLINIC

BEFORE...DURING...AFTER

Progress Report

Check to see where you are three times during this course....at the end of the....

- First session
- Fourth session
- Seventh session

If you had a complete physical, mental, relational and spiritual check up at the Mayo Clinic by doctors in these fields, what would they conclude about you. Record your pulse in each of these areas by putting a dot on the line below to indicate how you see yourself—1 being POOR and 10 being EXCELLENT health.

PHYSICALLY: I am feeling good physically. I stay in shape. Exercise regularly. Eat right. Sleep well. Enjoy life. Physically, I am...

Poor —————————————————— Excellent
  1 2 3 4 5 6 7 8 9 10

MENTALLY: I am feeling good about myself. I build myself up. I have some God-given abilities. Strengths. I like who I am. Mentally, I am...

Poor —————————————————— Excellent
  1 2 3 4 5 6 7 8 9 10

RELATIONALLY: I am feeling good about sharing myself with others. I make friends well. Deal with conflict. Reach out. Care. Forgive. Relationally, I am...

Poor —————————————————— Excellent
  1 2 3 4 5 6 7 8 9 10

SPIRITUALLY: I am feeling good about my relationship with God. I am getting my spiritual life together, putting God first. Spiritually, I am...

Poor —————————————————— Excellent
  1 2 3 4 5 6 7 8 9 10

Love the Lord your God with all your heart,
with all your soul...with all your mind,
and with all your strength...and
Love your neighbor as you love yourself.
Mark 12:30-31

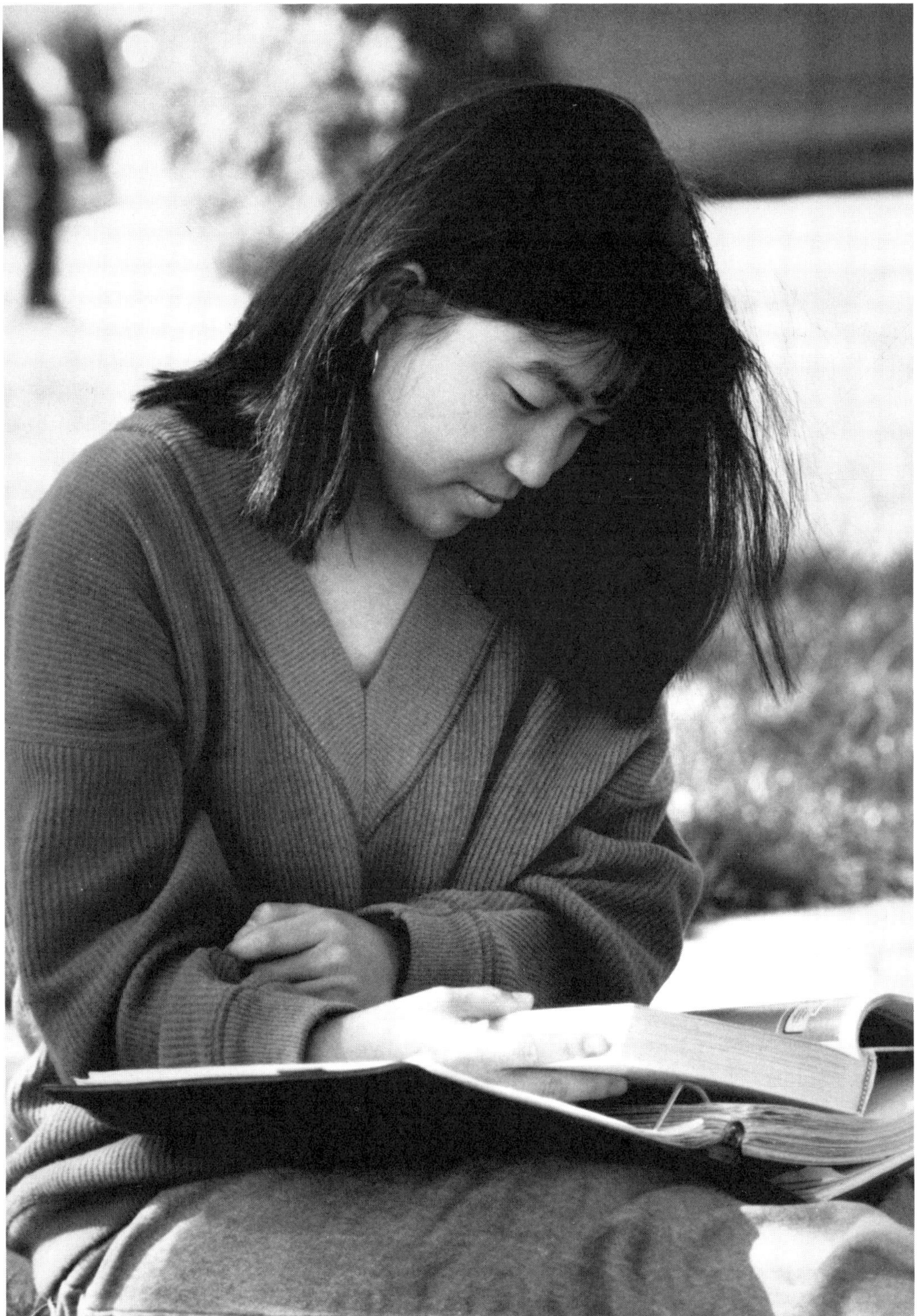

LEADER:
Before you start, read A Word to the Youth Leaders, on page 46.

SESSION 1
Holy Grail

WARM UP
Groups of 2
15 minutes

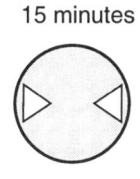

LEADER:
Pass out books. Explain teamwork principle. Explain diagrams on page 46 and theory behind 2's, 4's and 8's. Break into teams of 8's. Then, pair off in 2's for Warm Up. Read Introduction and call time after 15 minutes and move to the Bible Study.

Forced Choices

Introduction. Welcome to this course on choices. Over the next several sessions, you are going to be making a lot of choices. Choices about yourself. Your habits. Your values. Your priorities. And most of all, what you want to do with your life.

This program works like a sports training camp. In each session you will be put through a series of group-building exercises, starting out with groups of 2, then groups of 4 and finally a group of 8.

Over the time that you are in this course, you will have a chance to get to know each other real well. . .and learn how to help each other as a team.

Now, to get started, divide into groups of two and take this simple quiz below. With your partner, explain a little bit about yourself by choosing ONE of the two options on each line. For more fun, let your partner guess first.

I PREFER

staying up late . . . . getting up early
fast-food drive-in . . . . fancy restaurant
chicken . . . . pizza
playing football . . . . watching football
skiing in the mountains . . . . sunning by the sea
sports clothes . . . . grubbies
lots of friends . . . . one close friend

I WOULD CHOOSE

life of ease . . . . life of surprises
sitting on the bench   playing every game
on a winning team . . . . on a losing team
inherit a million . . . . make a million
have a job with lots of   have a job with lots
challenge/no security . . . . of security/no challenge
play inside the rules . . . . outside the rules

FEEDBACK: Let your partner respond by finishing these two sentences.

1. We are very much alike in our choices on. . .

2. We are different when it comes to. . .

5

BIBLE STUDY
Groups of 4
15-30 minutes

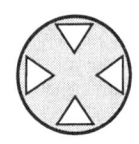

LEADER:
Put two 2's together to make 4's. Rearrange chairs. Read Introduction and scripture aloud. Save 30 minutes for last part—Caring.

The Pearl of Great Price

Introduction. The Bible study in this course will give you a chance to look at some of the stories in the Bible about choices. In this session, you will look at two parables that Jesus told about what you value most.

The Bible study is in two parts: (1) **Looking Into The Story**—about the story in the Bible, and (2) **My Own Story**—about your own experience. There is a discussion questionnaire with multiple-choice options for you to choose. There are no right or wrong answers. . .so you can feel free to share your opinions.

We recommend that you divide into groups of 4 for this Bible study—so that everyone can participate in the discussion. And be sure to save the last 20 to 30 minutes at the close of this session to make some important decisions about this course.

Now, move into groups of 4 and let someone read the Bible passage.

THE PARABLE OF THE HIDDEN TREASURE
44"The Kingdom of heaven is like this. A man happens to find a treasure hidden in a field. He covers it up again, and is so happy that he goes and sells everything he has, and then goes back and buys that field."

THE PARABLE OF THE PEARL
45"Also, the Kingdom of heaven is like this. A man is looking for fine pearls, 46and when he finds one that is unusually fine, he goes and sells everything he has, and buys that pearl."
                                                          Matthew 13:44-46

Looking Into the Story: In groups of 4, let one person answer question #1. The next person answer question #2. . .etc., until you have answered all four questions. Remember, there are no right or wrong answers. . .so feel free to share your opinion.

1. If the two people who found these treasures—the treasure in the field and the unusually fine pearl—met each other, what do you think would happen?
    a. they would want what the other person had
    b. they would argue about whose treasure was better
    c. they would have a good time swapping treasure stories
    d. they would become great friends because they would understand each other's joy

2. How long do you think it took for the person to decide to sell everything and buy the field?
    a. about one second
    b. a few hours—after all, he must have loved his possessions
    c. a few days—to get a loan to buy the field
    d. his whole life—because it probably took a whole lot of money to buy that field

3. In the second parable—pearl of great price—what motivated this person to sell everything to get the pearl?
   a. money—he was a buyer out to make a buck
   b. satisfaction—he was a merchant but he wanted this pearl for himself
   c. long-term investment—he knew this pearl was unusually fine and would go up in value
   d. recognition—he wanted to wear it so that people would comment on it
   e. happiness—it would bring him joy

4. What do you think his friends said when he showed up at school without nice clothes, no bike, no car, no computer, no CD collection, no acoustical guitar and no money set aside for college. . .and showed his friends one little pearl?
   a. so. . .like, when did you say you were going to the "shrink"?
   b. what did you say your girl's name was?
   c. you're bringing this to our school—with no armed guard?
   d. you sold all that neat stuff for something you can only look at?
   e. that's cool—where can I get one?

My Own Story: Note the change in the way you share. Everyone answers question #1. Then, everyone answers question #2. . .etc. through the questions.

1. What is the most important thing in your life right now?
   a. girls/boys
   b. sports
   c. fun
   d. making money
   e. friends
   f. church
   g. school
   h. being popular
   i. getting into college
   j. my possessions

2. If you had to sell all of your possessions to buy this pearl of great price, what would you sell. . .first and last?
   a. my bike/car
   b. my computer
   c. my best clothes
   d. my date book with all the phone numbers
   e. my musical instrument/CD player
   f. my position on the team
   g. my scrap book/hobby
   h. my bedroom furniture/valuables
   i. my music tapes & CD's
   j. my savings account that I have set aside for college

3. On the list in question 1, what has gone up in value in the last 12 months? What has gone down in value? (Mark + or -)

4. On the list above, what would your parents like for you to value more? Value less? (Mark P+ or P-)

5. What is likely to be more important to you five years from now? (Mark 5+)

6. How much does your commitment to the Kingdom of heaven influence your choices in life right now?
   a. a whole lot
   b. a little
   c. not a whole lot
   d. I'll let you know later

7. How do you feel about being in this course and talking about personal stuff with those in your youth group?
   a. I love it
   b. I have a few reservations
   c. I'm scared
   d. I'm not the talkative type
   e. I'll let you know next week

8. If you do join this program, what do you want clearly understood by those in the group?
   a. I can say "I pass" on anything I don't want to talk about
   b. anything that is said in the group is not repeated outside of the group
   c. religion is not going to be "pushed" on me
   d. I can get out of the group after this course is over
   e. if we are going to be a team—everybody must be committed

CARING
Teams of 8
15-20 minutes

Team Sign Up

Introduction: Now is the time to decide what you want to get out of this course. For yourself. Your team. And to agree on the ground rules for teamwork. Follow these four steps.

Step 1: Check in. Turn to page 3 and let everyone on your team explain where they are right now in these areas of their life. (You will have a chance to retake this test half-way through and again at the close of the course to see where you have changed).

LEADER:
If you have more than ten to twelve, form groups of 8 by bringing two groups of 4 together. This group of 8 will stay together for the rest of this program—and meet together at the beginning and at the close of each session.

Step 2: Expectations. Give everyone a chance to share the top two things they would like to get out of this course, using the list below:

___ to have fun
___ to talk about the real stuff in my life
___ to get to know the Bible
___ to get closer as a youth group
___ to go out and do something
___ to reach out to other kids at school
___ to grow in my faith
___ hanging out with my friends
___ other:_____

Step 3: Ground Rules. What are one or two things on the list below that you would like to include in the ground rules for being in this course? See if you can agree on these?

_____ATTENDANCE: I will be at the meetings for the six sessions except in case of emergency.

_____CONFIDENTIALITY: I will keep anything that is said at the meetings in confidence.

_____PRAYER: I will pray for the others on this team.

_____REACH OUT: I will invite others from school and church to join our group.

_____MISSION PROJECT: I would like to see our team commit to a mission project at the close of this course.

_____PARTY: I would like to see us celebrate this course together at the close with a party or retreat.

_____ACCOUNTABILITY: I would like to see us report in each week on our spiritual walk with Christ.

LEADER:
At the close of this session, bring all of the teams together to reinforce the commitment—to be present every session.

Step 4: Prayer Partner. Inside of your team, choose one or two others to conclude this meeting. . .and every meeting for the next six sessions. . .with a time of prayer. Before you pray, "report" on how you are feeling. . .and how you want your prayer partner to pray for you this week. THEN, CALL DURING THE WEEK TO ASK "HOW'S IT GOING?"

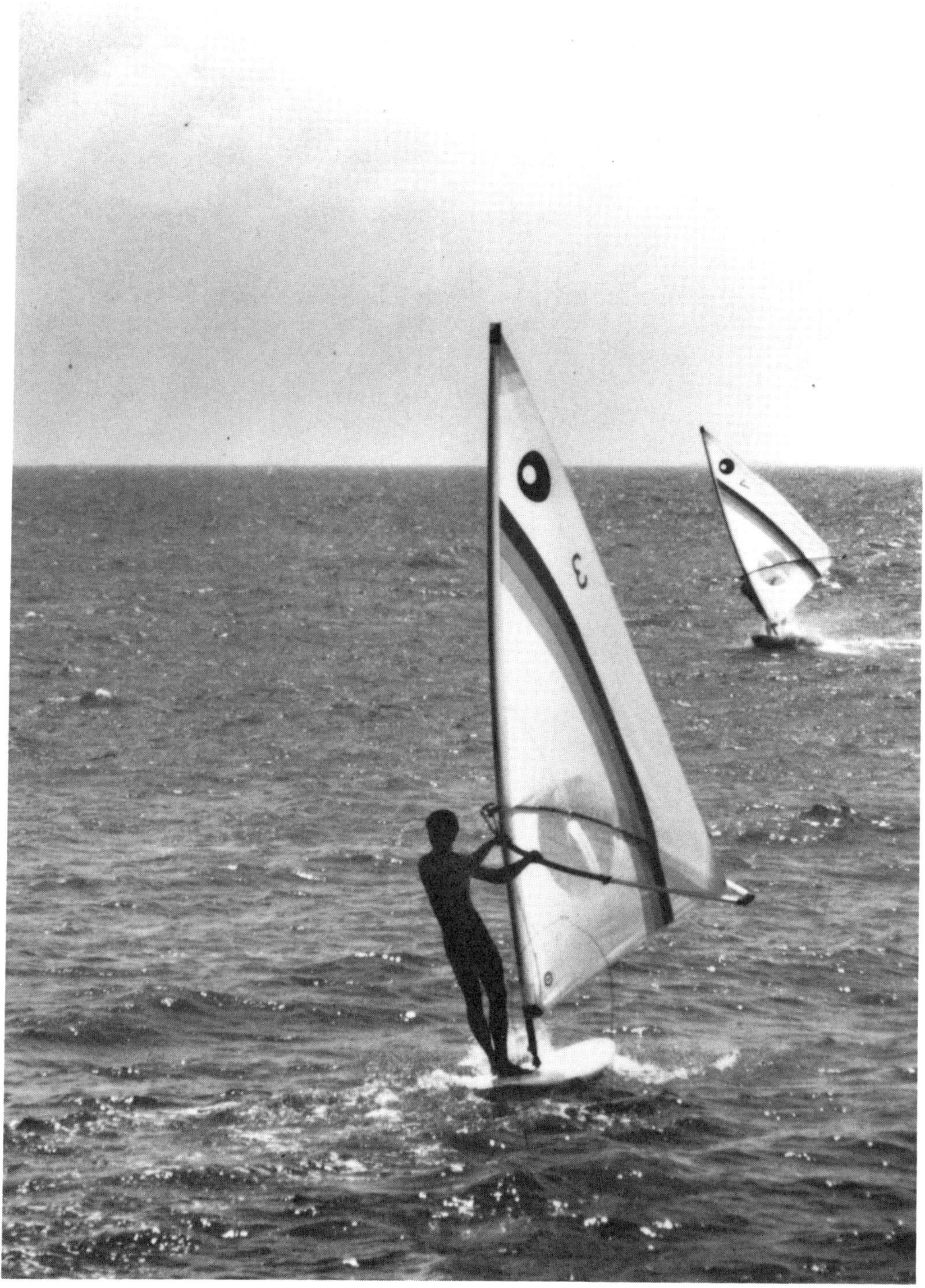

SESSION 2
Possessions

WARM UP
Groups of 2
15 minutes

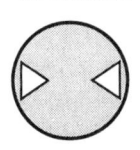

LEADER:
Recap the last session. Repeat the teamwork principles. Ask teams of 8 to divide into 2's—not the same person as last session.

Silent Auction

Introduction. This session is about values and possessions—the things that you value in your life.

To get started, get together with one person from your team (not the same person as last session) and go to a silent auction together. First, read over the list of items and write down a bid in the left column that you would bid on this item. You have a total of $1,000 that you can use to bid at this auction and you have to bid something on every item—with the lowest bid being $10. With the money that you have left, you can spread it over the items that you want. For instance you might put down $300 for "good relationship with my parents" because you want that item very much.

After you have jotted down your bids in silence, break the silence and find out which one of you won each item and write this person's name in the right column.

YOUR BID   WINNER

$_____ Season tickets for your favorite pro team   _____
$_____ A better looking body with no work out   _____
$_____ CD Player, color TV in your bedroom   _____
$_____ Fastest car in town   _____
$_____ Date with Miss/Mr. America   _____
$_____ Complete new wardrobe of latest fashions   _____
$_____ Two-week vacation with a friend in Hawaii   _____
$_____ Mountain bike, top of the line   _____
$_____ Assurance of a permanent job when you graduate   _____
$_____ Tickets to your favorite rock group in concert   _____
$_____ Rookie year football card of Joe Montana   _____
$_____ Picture taken with Kevin Kostner   _____
$_____ Good relationship with my parents   _____

BIBLE STUDY
Groups of 4
15-30 minutes

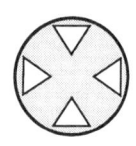

LEADER
Combine two 2's to make 4's. Read Introduction and Scripture. Call time 20 minutes before closing time.

Rich and Foolish

Introduction. A lot of people think that Jesus had it in for rich people. . . .and they often refer to this parable about a Rich Fool. However, this parable was not said to a rich person, but to a guy who didn't have a whole lot of money but was as greedy as a rich person and who wanted all the things that the rich have. Listen to the story.

Then, move into groups of four and discuss the questionnaire. It is in two parts: (1) **Looking Into The Story**—about the Bible story, and (2) **My Own Story**—about your own life. There are no right or wrong answers in the questionnaire, so feel free to speak up.

Be sure to save the last 20 minutes at the close for the caring time.

THE PARABLE OF THE RICH FOOL

¹³A man in the crowd said to Jesus, "Teacher, tell my brother to divide with me the property our father left us." ¹⁴Jesus answered him, "Friend, who gave me the right to judge or to divide the property between you two?" ¹⁵And he went on to say to them all, "Watch out and guard yourselves from every kind of greed; because your true life is not made up of the things you own, no matter how rich you may be."

¹⁶Then Jesus told them this parable: "There was once a rich man who had land which bore good crops. ¹⁷He began to think to himself, 'I don't have a place to keep all my crops. What can I do? ¹⁸This is what I will do,' he told himself; 'I will tear down my barns and build bigger ones, where I will store the grain and all my other goods. ¹⁹Then I will say to myself, Lucky man! You have all the good things you need for many years. Take life easy, eat, drink, and enjoy yourself!' ²⁰But God said to him, 'You fool! This very night you will have to give up your life; then who will get all these things you have kept for yourself?' "

²¹And Jesus concluded, "This is how it is with those who pile up riches for themselves, but are not rich in God's sight."

Luke 12:13-21

Looking Into The Story: In groups of 4, let one person answer question #1, the next person answer question #2, etc. around your group. There are no right or wrong answers.

1. If the Rich Fool in the parable (you can call him George or Georgia Megabucks) went to your school, how would he/she dress?
    a. designer clothes/latest fashion
    b. regular clothes/Nike shoes
    c. grubbies—when you are that rich, it is stylish to look trashy
    d. other:_____

2. If George or Georgia Megabucks wanted to impress the kids in your school with his or her money, what would they do instead of build barns?
   a. show up in a new sports car—convertible
   b. throw a big party for his or her friends and bring in a live band
   c. take their friends to his/her little house in Aspen for a ski weekend
   d. buy girlfriend or boyfriend a friendship ring—one carat diamond
   e. other:_____

3. How would you describe the rich man in the parable? (choose two words)
   a. clever
   b. secure
   c. show off
   d. screwed up
   e. immature
   f. brilliant
   g. unhappy

4. How do you react to the teaching, "your true life is not made up of things you own, no matter how rich you may be?"
   a. sounds like the teaching of someone who was poor and jealous
   b. it's what a preacher is supposed to say
   c. yeah, well my friends with nice cars and clothes sure <u>seem</u> happy!
   d. yeah, but being rich can get you friends, and friends <u>are</u> what life is about
   e. it's true—the best things in life are free

5. Work together as a group to fill out this form obituary about George/Georgia Megabucks for the local newspaper about his/her death.

   ❑ Last night George/Georgia Megabucks passed away suddenly. George/Georgia was well known in the community for his/her. . .

   ❑ George/Georgia Megabucks used his/her vast wealth for. . .

   ❑ Before his/her untimely death, George/Georgia Megabucks was engaged in. . .

   ❑ His/her attitude toward life was best expressed by his/her. . .

   ❑ This timeless servant spent his/her whole life. . .

   ❑ A memorial service for George/Georgia will be held at. . .

   ❑ In his/her honor a special fund is being started to benefit. . .

My Own Story: Note the shift in the sharing instructions. Go around on question #1 and let everyone answer the question. Then, go around again on question #2. . . . etc., through the questions.

1. If you had been a friend of the rich man in this parable, how would you have acted toward him?
   a. kissed up to him so he would invite me to his parties
   b. snubbed him just to show everyone I don't care about money
   c. treated him like everyone else
   d. witnessed to him about Christ
   e. shown him how to relax and just enjoy life
   f. other:_____

2. If you suddenly came into money, what would you do with it?
   a. quit school—travel the world
   b. buy a car/motorcycle
   c. not let any of my friends know
   d. keep doing the things I am doing now
   e. share it with friends
   f. throw a party for friends
   g. give it away to the needy
   h. other:_____

3. Up to this point in your life, what would you feel have been your top three accomplishments? Check below.
   ___ learning to tie my own shoes in preschool
   ___ surviving to this point in life
   ___ getting good grades in school
   ___ my athletic achievements
   ___ making some great friends
   ___ getting a girlfriend/boyfriend
   ___ helping a friend with a serious problem
   ___ learning to play an instrument well
   ___ being elected a student or youth group leader
   ___ sticking up for my values
   ___ I can't think of anything I've accomplished
   ___ other:_____

4. If you should die today, what would your friends say about you in the newspaper? Finish the sentences below with the first thing that comes to mind. If the others in your group want to help you, let them speak up.

   ❏ Last night (fill in your name) died suddenly.

   ❏ He/she will always be remembered in the youth group at church for their. . .

   ❏ He/she always had time for. . .

   ❏ He/she felt that possessions like clothes, radios and personal items were. . .

   ❏ He/she treated people like. . .

   ❏ On the tombstone, the words of a song are inscribed. They are. . .

CARING
Teams of 8
15-20 minutes

LEADER:
Bring teams back together for Step 1 and 2. Then, Step 3 with prayer partners for this course.

Team Check-In: How's It Going?

Introduction: After two sessions in this program, stop the camera and evaluate what you think about the program. . .and what you would like to change.

Regather with your team and go over the questions together. Be sure to save the last few minutes to be with your prayer partner (Step 3).

Step 1: Check Your Pulse. What do you appreciate most about this course? Go around and let everyone share one or two things.

___ fun times
___ studying the Bible
___ close relationships
___ feeling like I belong
___ sharing our problems
___ praying for each other
___ reaching out to others
___ other:_____

Step 2: I Wish. If you could have one wish for this program, what would be your wish? Finish the sentence, I wish we could have. . .

___ more sharing about each other
___ more time for Bible Study
___ more fun
___ more reach out
___ more trips
___ less joking around
___ less gossip
___ less study
___ other:_____

Step 3: Prayer Partner. Get together with your prayer partner that you started with last week, and describe the last seven days in your life as a weather report. Then, close in prayer for each other. Finish the sentence, "This past week has been. . ."

❏ Blue sky, bright sunshine all week long—NO PROBLEMS
❏ Partly cloudy most of the week—A FEW PROBLEMS AT HOME
❏ Severe storms all week long
❏ mixed—some days sunny, some days cloudy
❏ warming trend—getting better
❏ tornado/hurricane—DISASTERS!
❏ other:_____

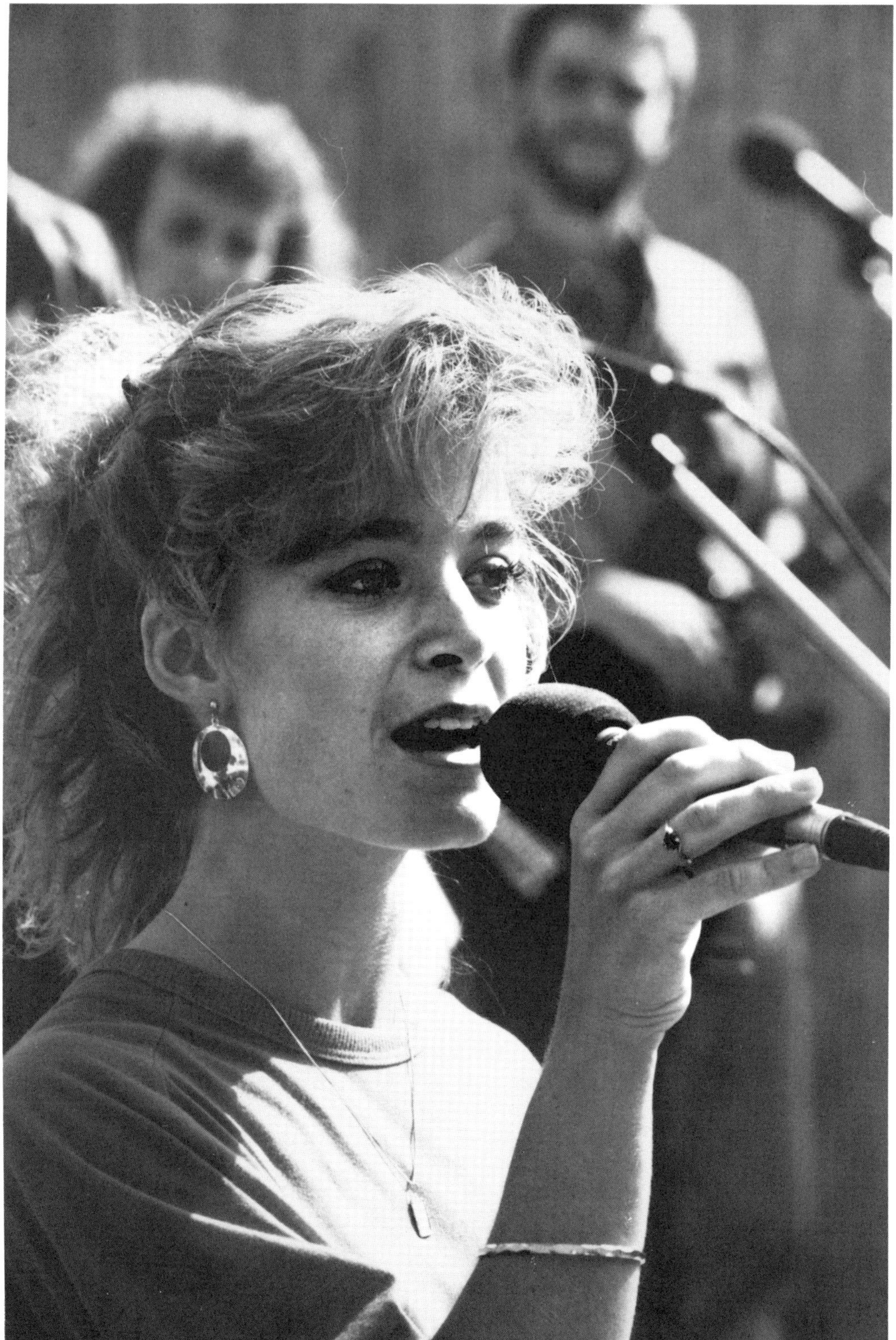

SESSION 3
Using Your Abilities

WARM UP
Groups of 2
15 minutes

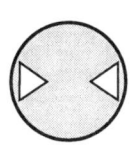

My Daily Routine

Introduction. Everybody gets 24 hours a day. It's how you use it that counts. In this session, you are going to look at the way you spend your time—your schedule.

To get started, get together with someone that you have not been with from your team and explain your daily routine. . .finishing the sentences below.

When you are finished, let your partner respond to what you have said by finishing the two sentences under FEEDBACK.

Then, reverse the roles and let your partner explain to you their daily routine.

IN A USUAL DAY. . .

1. I get up around. . .
2. I usually take a (shower or bath).
3. It takes me about _____ minutes to dress and get ready.
4. For breakfast I usually have. . .
5. I leave for school around. . .
6. For lunch, I have. . .
7. I get home from school around. . .
8. To unwind, I usually. . .
9. If I have some free time, I usually. . .
10. I eat supper around. . .
11. If I don't have any homework, I usually. . .
12. If I watch TV I usually look at. . .
13. I usually go to bed around. . .
14. I put my clothes on the. . . (floor/chair)
15. It takes me about _____ minutes to fall asleep.

FEEDBACK:

1. We are very much alike in our routine when it comes to. . .

2. We are different in our routine when it comes to. . .

BIBLE STUDY
Groups of 4
15-30 minutes

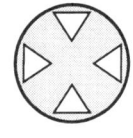

The Hidden Talent

Introduction. In the last session you studied someone who made money the most important thing in his life. Jesus called him a "fool". In this session, you are going to study a guy who didn't use the money he was given. Jesus calls this guy "useless".

As you listen to the Bible story, see if you can figure out the difference. . . and what Jesus might say to you about the way you use your time and money.

The questionnaire is in two parts: (1) **Looking Into The Story**—about the Bible story, and (2) **My Own Story**—about your own life. Now, move into groups of four and get set for the Bible study.

Be sure to save the last 20 minutes at the close for caring time.

THE PARABLE OF THE THREE SERVANTS

[14] "At that time the Kingdom of heaven will be like this. Once there was a man who was about to leave home on a trip; he called his servants and put them in charge of his property. [15] He gave to each one according to his ability: to one he gave five thousand gold coins, to another he gave two thousand, and to another he gave one thousand. Then he left on his trip. [16] The servant who had received five thousand coins went at once and invested his money and earned another five thousand. [17] In the same way the servant who had received two thousand coins earned another two thousand. [18] But the servant who had received one thousand coins went off, dug a hole in the ground, and hid his master's money.

[19] "After a long time the master of those servants came back and settled accounts with them. [20] The servant who had received five thousand coins came in and handed over the other five thousand. 'You gave me five thousand coins, sir,' he said, 'Look! Here are another five thousand that I have earned.' [21] 'Well done, you good and faithful servant!' said his master. 'You have been faithful in managing small amounts, so I will put you in charge of large amounts. Come on in and share my happiness!' [22] Then the servant who had been given two thousand coins came in and said, 'You gave me two thousand coins, sir. Look! Here are another two thousand that I have earned.' [23] 'Well done, you good and faithful servant!' said his master. 'You have been faithful in managing small amounts, so I will put you in charge of large amounts. Come on in and share my happiness!' [24] Then the servant who had received one thousand coins came in and said, 'Sir, I know you are a hard man; you reap harvests where you did not plant, and you gather crops where you did not scatter seed. [25] I was afraid, so I went off and hid your money in the ground. Look! Here is what belongs to you.' [26] 'You bad and lazy servant!' his master said. 'You knew, did you, that I reap harvests where I did not plant, and gather crops where I did not scatter seed? [27] Well, then, you should have deposited my money in the bank, and I would have received it all back with interest when I returned. [28] Now, take the money away from him and give it to the one who has ten thousand coins. [29] For to every person who

has something, even more will be given, and he will have more than enough; but the person who has nothing, even the little that he has will be taken away from him. ³⁰As for this useless servant—throw him outside in the darkness; there he will cry and gnash his teeth.' "

Matthew 25:14-30

Looking Into The Story: In groups of 4, let the first person answer question #1, the next person question #2, etc. . . .around the group.

1. Which of the three servants in this story is most like you?
    a. the one who was given 5,000 coins—I get a big allowance
    b. the one who was given 2,000 coins—just an average kid, doing my part
    c. the one who was given 1,000 coins—I always get the short end!

2. Why do you think this servant dug a hole and hid his money rather than investing it?
    a. he was afraid
    b. he didn't know what to do
    c. he was not used to taking responsibility
    d. he had a sister who was smarter than he was
    e. he grew up in a family that expected him to take responsibility and he rebelled
    f. he didn't know that the consequences for laziness were going to be this bad

3. Why do you think the owner was so hard on him?
    a. he was in training to be a school principal
    b. he was greedy
    c. you have to be hard-nosed in the business world
    d. he was like a football coach—he got angry when people didn't do their best
    e. he wanted the guy to learn to be a risk taker

4. If you had been the owner, what would you have done to this guy?
    a. taken his driver's license away
    b. made him go to a Saturday class on investing
    c. assigned him to a recovery group for unmotivated kids
    d. given him another chance—with another one thousand coins
    e. been even harder on this guy than the owner was and hope he would learn some responsibility

5. Do you think it was fair for the owner to give less money to one of his servants and then judge him for not doing anything with it?
    a. absolutely, the owner can do anything he wants
    b. well, I don't play that way
    c. that is life—you play with what you are given
    d. this is not the point in this story

My Own Story: Note the shift in instructions for sharing. Everyone in your group answers question #1. Then, go around again on question #2, etc.

1. When have you been entrusted with a lot of money or an important task?
    a. at my job when I handle money
    b. I care for my brother/sister when my parents aren't home
    c. in other responsibilities given to me at home
    d. in responsibilities given to me at church
    e. in responsibilities given to me at school
    f. nowhere

2. How do you feel when you are given a lot of responsibility?
    a. nervous—I hope I don't blow it!
    b. proud—people believe in me!
    c. overwhelmed—I'm too young for this!
    d. confident—I can handle it!

3. When you don't handle a responsibility as well as you should, how do the adults in charge generally react? In front of the responses below, mark "P" for how your parent(s) react, "T" for how your teachers normally react, "W" for how people react at your job if you have one, and "C" for how adult leaders at church react. Then place an arrow by the reaction you wish more people should have to such failures:

    ___ they put me down

    ___ they punish me

    ___ they stop trusting me

    ___ they tell me how to do better

    ___ they give the responsibility to someone else

    ___ they tell me what I did <u>right</u>

    ___ they yell and scream

    ___ they ignore it

    ___ they act like I did it right when I know I didn't

4. What would you say that you need to do to become a more responsible "servant"?
    a. have more confidence I can do what is asked of me
    b. take my responsibilities more seriously
    c. trust in God to help me
    d. get more encouragement from others
    e. responsible?—I just want to have fun!

CARING
Teams of 8
15-20 minutes

How Do You Feel About Your Team?

Introduction: You have been together for three sessions. Take your pulse on how you feel about your group. Steps 1 and 2 are for your team together. Step 3 is with your prayer partner.

Step 1: Report In. If you could compare your involvement in this program to somewhere on the diagram below, where would you be:

- In the grandstand—for spectators—just looking on
- On the bench—on the team—but not playing
- On the playing field—where the action is
- In the showers—on the injury list

```
┌─────────────────────────────┐
│        GRANDSTAND           │
│      (For spectators)       │
└─────────────────────────────┘

        ┌──────────────┐
        │ BENCH (team) │
        └──────────────┘

┌─────────────────────────────┐  ┌─────┐
│       PLAYING FIELD         │  │ THE │
│    (Where the action is)    │  │SHOW-│
│                             │  │ERS  │
└─────────────────────────────┘  └─────┘
```

Step 2: Teamwork. How would you describe the way you work together as a team in sports language? Finish the sentence: When we play together we're...

- jittery—like in our first game
- learning to trust each person on the team
- awkward—but we're improving
- fourth and goal to go—let's get it done!

Step 3: Prayer Partner. Get together with your prayer partner for this program and check to see how it went last week. Then, spend a little time in prayer for each other. Start off by picking a number from 1 to 10—1 being TERRIBLE and 10 being GREAT—to describe how last week went.

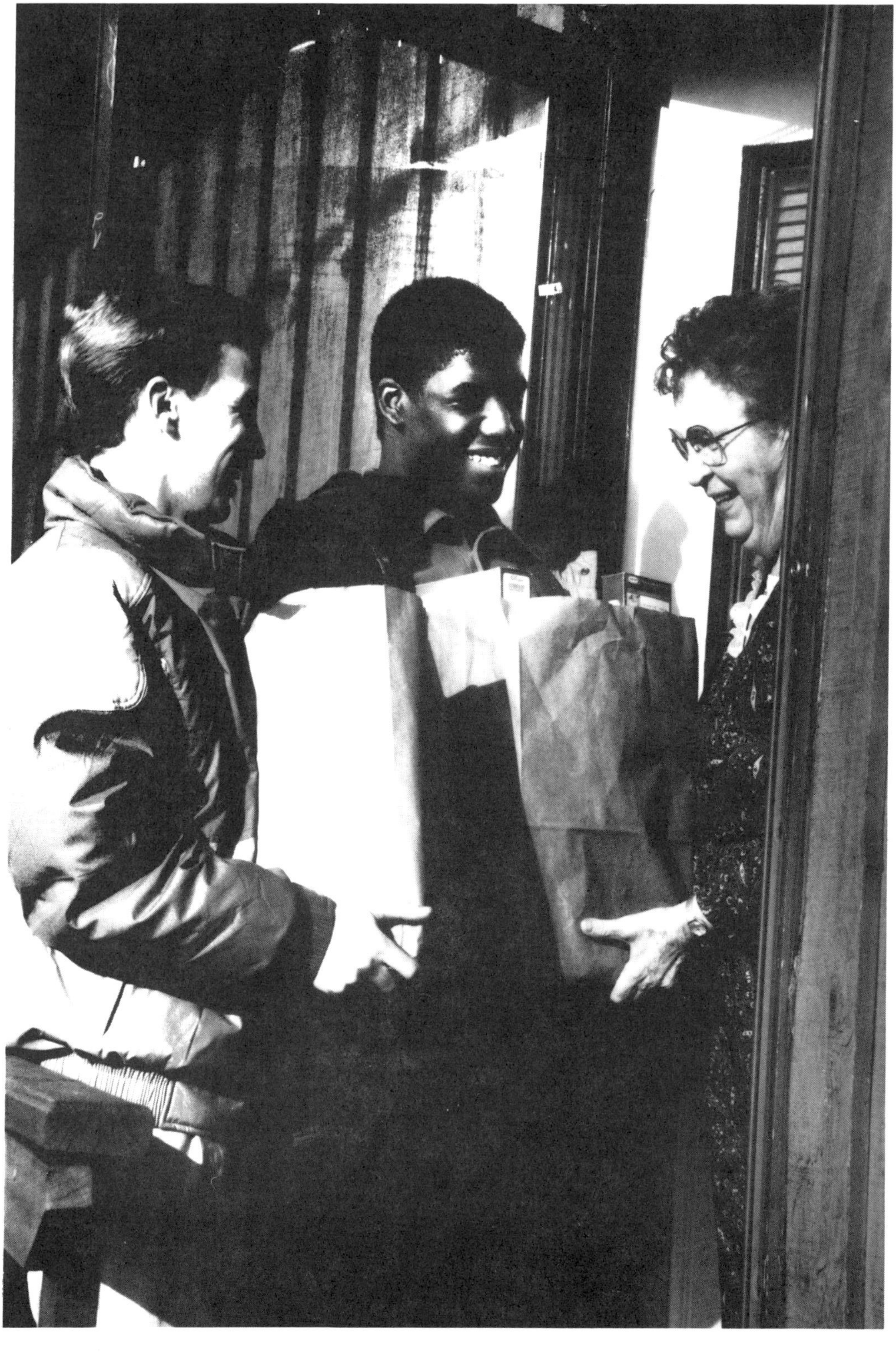

SESSION 4
Concerns / Causes

WARM UP
Groups of 2
15 minutes

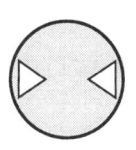

Lay It On the Line

Introduction. In this session, you are going to talk about your concerns and the causes that you believe in.

To get started, get together with one other person on your team and explain where you stand on these issues—somewhere in between the two extremes. For instance, on SMOKING you might put the dot in the middle, because you are equal distance between the two people on smoking.

Both of you take the first category. Then, move to the second category and explain that, etc. . .through the list.

ON FEMINISM
A woman's place is   A woman's place is in the House. . .
in the home _____of Representatives!

ON LAW AND ORDER
Lock the "critters" up _____Educate and Rehabilitate them

RESPECT FOR TRADITIONAL VALUES
God, Country and Family _____Nothing is sacred

ON ABORTION
Keep your hands off my body _____We are guardians of the unborn

ON CONDOMS
Kids have got to learn to protect   They encourage
themselves _____promiscuity

ON PORNOGRAPHY
It's a first amendment   We can't let such "freedom"
right_____destroy society

ON SMOKING
Smokers have rights too _____Your right to smoke stops at my nose

BIBLE STUDY
Groups of 4
15-30 minutes

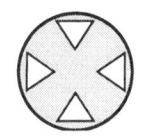

Shine Your Light

Introduction. The parables of salt and light have lost some of the impact today because salt is so easy to come by and electric lights have solved the problem of light. But in Bible times, salt was a precious commodity and hard to get. As you will see in the parable, it was a powerful change agent for food until it lost its strength. Then, it was no good.

And "light" was a luxury in a time when you sat in the dark a lot. Light could turn a rainy day into a blessing.

Jesus used these two metaphors to talk about influence. Move into groups of four. Then, listen to the Scripture and discuss the questionnaire below. Be sure to save the last 20 minutes at the close for the Caring Time.

> [13]"**You are like salt for the whole human race. But if salt loses its saltiness, there is no way to make it salty again. It has become worthless, so it is thrown out and people trample on it.**
>
> [14]"**You are like light for the whole world. A city built on a hill cannot be hid.** [15]**No one lights a lamp and puts it under a bowl; instead it is put on the lampstand, where it gives light for everyone in the house.** [16]**In the same way your light must shine before people, so that they will see the good things you do and praise your Father in heaven.**
>
> Matthew 5:13-16

Looking Into The Story: In groups of four, let the first person answer question #1, the next person question #2, etc. . .around the group.

1. When Jesus told us to be like salt, he was meaning. . .
   a. we should give everyone high blood pressure
   b. we are to bring flavor to life
   c. we are to preserve values that otherwise could be lost
   d. we should remain true to the role God gives us in life
   e. we should stick to popcorn and french fries

2. What is the significance of the fact that people trample on salt that has lost its saltiness?
   a. people on bland diets get testy
   b. if you don't stand up for what you believe, people walk on you
   c. if you don't do what God has called you to do, you lose your worth
   d. if people can't use you, they throw you out

3. Which of the following do you feel would be the best ways for you to "let your light shine before people"? (choose two)
   ___ carry my Bible to school
   ___ witness to my friends
   ___ speak out when racist or sexist jokes are told
   ___ get involved regularly in helping people in need
   ___ invite friends to church
   ___ show love to kids who are not part of my group
   ___ help the outcast kids at school

4. What is the difference between letting your "light shine before people" and bragging about how good or religious you are?

My Own Story: Go around on question #1 and let everyone choose their top three causes to get involved in and explain why. Then, go around again on question #2, etc. . . .through the questions.

1. Which of these causes do you believe so strongly in that you would get involved or take a stand? Choose the top three.

    ___ **Ecology:** Your neighborhood is being polluted by smoke stacks from an industry that employs many townspeople. To close the plant would throw them out of work.

    ___ **Abortion:** You know that a clinic in your community is performing abortions.

    ___ **Motorcycle helmets and seat belts:** You are forced to take safety measures for your own protection—which you feel is an infringement on your personal freedom.

    ___ **Firearms:** In your community the deaths from gunshot wounds have doubled in the last five years because of unrestricted sale of firearms.

    ___ **Smoking:** Many public places are crowded with people smoking. The Surgeon General has determined that smoke is harmful to anyone exposed to it.

    ___ **Equality:** A firm in your community has a history of not hiring a particular ethnic group. You are asked to join a picket line protesting their discriminatory tactics.

    ___ **Discrimination:** Your friend has been refused a job because she is a woman. She has asked you to join in a protest against the company.

    ___ **Pornography:** The local video store is renting hard core to minors under the counter.

    ___ **Hospital aids:** The local hospital has appealed for volunteers to empty bed pans and serve in the recovery room.

    ___ **Conservation:** You have learned that ranchers in your state have killed some eagles by placing poison in sheep carcasses.

    ___ **Evangelism:** A famous preacher is holding a crusade in your town and you have been asked to bring kids from your school to the meetings.

More on next page

___ **World hunger:** World Vision is sponsoring a 25-mile walk for the hungry and you are asked to participate and get your neighbors to sponsor you.

___ **Public prayer**: You are asked to say the opening prayer at the Thanksgiving Day football game in front of the whole community.

2. Go back over the list above and explain where your values and choices have changed—using these questions:

    • what issue would your parents get involved in

    • what issue has been more important to you in the last year

    • what issue is something the church should not get involved in

    • what issue will become more important to you when you have children

    • what issue would Jesus probably "turn over a few tables" for

3. What causes do you get involved in? Finish the sentence by choosing ONE in each category: "I tend to get involved in causes that. . ."

    • threaten my own life and self interests _____ threaten the lives of others

    • involve physical health and well being _____ involve spiritual health and well being

    • my friends are concerned about _____ my family are concerned about

4. How much does your relationship with Jesus Christ influence the causes you get involved in?
    a. a whole lot
    b. some
    c. not much
    d. sorry you asked

5. As far as being "salt" and "light" in the world, how would you describe yourself right now?
    a. still trying to figure out where I stand on issues
    b. I know where I stand, but I'm not getting involved
    c. I'm in the game, but I'm playing defense
    d. I'm doing everything I know to do
    e. I'll let you know in a few days

CARING
Teams of 8
15-20 minutes

Mid-Course Affirmation

Introduction. It's half time. Time for a break. Get together with your team of 8 (or the whole group if you have less than twelve) and evaluate your experience so far.

Here are two options. The second option is more risky, but a lot more personal if you have grown to appreciate each other.

Option 1: Half-time Progress Report. Turn to page three and let everyone report any growth in your life since being in this program.

Option 2: Appreciation Time. Ask one person on your team to sit in silence while the others share one thing that you have come to appreciate about this person. Finish one of these sentences:

Since being in your group, I have come to see you as...

or

Since being in your group, I have come to appreciate you for your...

After you have gone around your group on the first person, ask the next person to sit in silence while the others finish the sentence on this person...etc. around the group.

This is called "strength bombardment" or "appreciation bombardment." You've done a lot of talking about yourself during this program. Now you will have a chance to hear what the others on your team have learned about you. Get set for a beautiful experience in AFFIRMATION.

If you don't know how to get started, look over the list below and pick out a word or two words that help describe what you see in this person...and tell them so.

I SEE YOU AS VERY...:

loyal	quiet	dependable	daring
fun	gorgeous	resourceful	lovable
friendly	childlike	cheerful	steady
irresistible	sensitive	meditative	spiritual
caring	unsinkable	warm	dedicated
gentle	rugged	awesome	emerging
strong	untamed	playful	crazy
courageous	special	thoughtful	energetic
encouraging	beautiful	persistent	confident

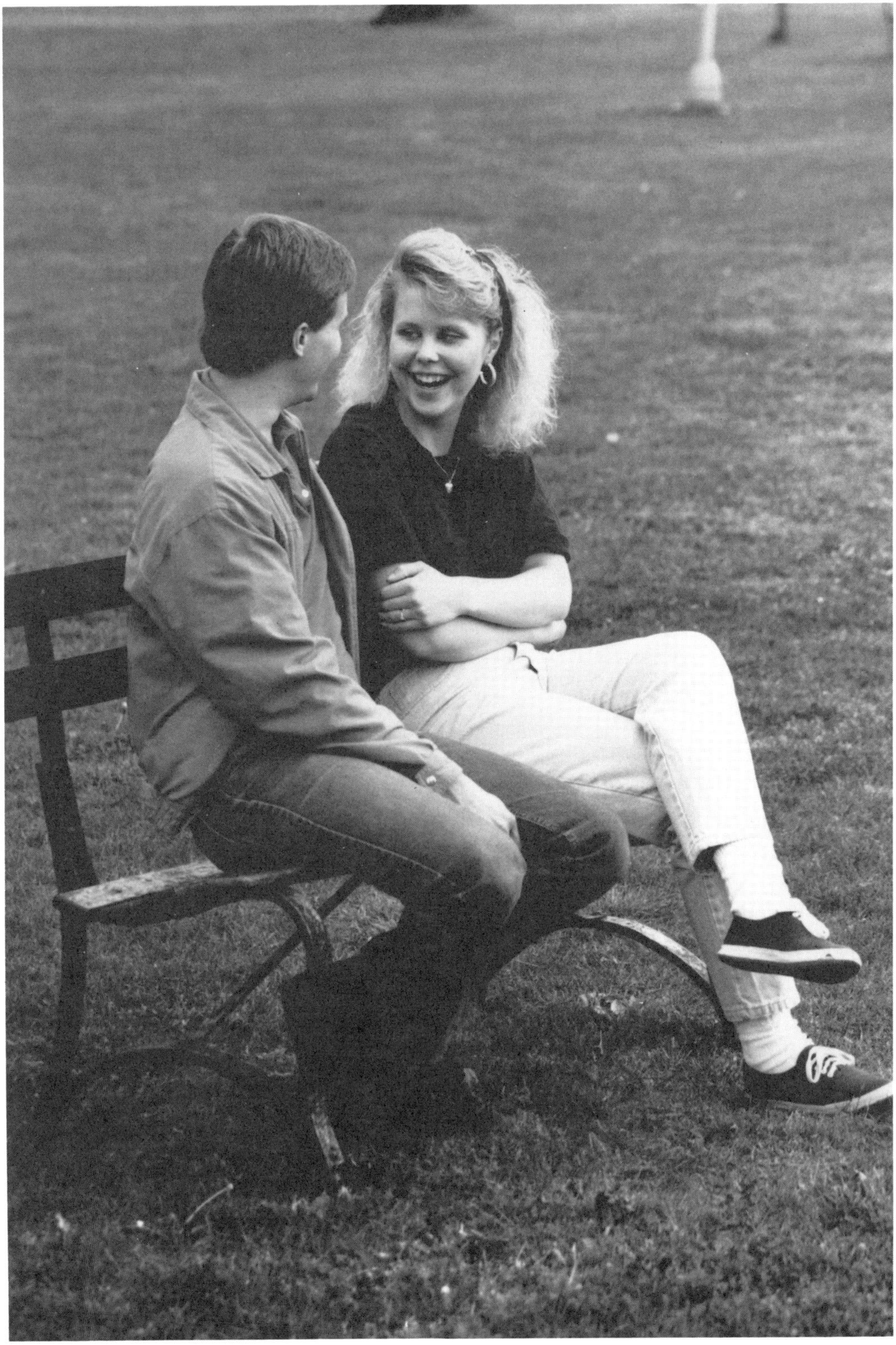

SESSION 5
Sex

WARM UP
Groups of 2
15 minutes

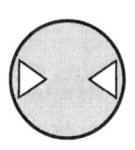

Fantasy Wedding

Introduction. Congratulations. You are just about to marry a super rich millionaire. . .and you can plan the most expensive wedding you want. What are you going to plan?

Get together with one other person from your team and let this person be your private secretary as you plan this wedding. Your partner will ask you the questions below and you can think a moment before you answer. Remember, money is not a problem. Dream big.

1. What country of the world would you like to be married in?
2. Where in this country would you like to be married?
3. If you could fly in your special music group for this wedding, who would you like to invite?
4. Who would you like to invite to the wedding?
5. Who is going to perform the ceremony?
6. Who is going to be your special soloist?
7. What favorite song would you like for this person to sing?
8. Who is going to officiate/pronounce the vows?
9. Where are you going to have the reception?
10. Where are you going to go for your honeymoon?
11. How are you going to get there?
12. Where would you like to live when you get back?
13. How many children would you like to have?
14. Boys or girls?
15. Now—if they were not already married—what famous person would you like to marry?

FEEDBACK: About your partner's wedding plans, finish these two sentences.

1. I must say, your wedding is going to be a . . .

2. If the famous person that you mentioned refused to marry you, I would like to nominate another famous person by the name of. . .

BIBLE STUDY
Groups of 4
15-30 minutes

Joseph & Potiphar's Wife

Introduction. In this session you will study what one person, a young person by the name of Joseph, did about temptation.

Joseph was one of twelve brothers. He was favored by his father, which caused his brothers to hate him...and sell him to some Egyptians...who sold him to Potiphar, the captain of Pharaoh's palace guard.

Listen to the story of what happened...and then discuss the questionnaire in groups of 4. Make sure to save the last 20-30 minutes for the Caring Time at the close.

JOSEPH AND POTIPHAR'S WIFE

[1] Now the Ishmaelites had taken Joseph to Egypt and sold him to Potiphar, one of the king's officers, who was the captain of the palace guard. [2] The Lord was with Joseph and made him successful. He lived in the house of his Egyptian master, [3] who saw that the Lord was with Joseph and had made him successful in everything he did. [4] Potiphar was pleased with him and made him his personal servant; so he put him in charge of his house and everything he owned. [5] From then on, because of Joseph the Lord blessed the household of the Egyptian and everything that he had in his house and in his fields. [6] Potiphar turned over everything he had to the care of Joseph and did not concern himself with anything except the food he ate.

Joseph was well-built and good-looking, [7] and after a while his master's wife began to desire Joseph and asked him to go to bed with her. [8] He refused and said to her, "Look, my master does not have to concern himself with anything in the house, because I am here. He has put me in charge of everything he has. [9] I have as much authority in this house as he has, and he has not kept back anything from me except you. How then could I do such an immoral thing and sin against God?" [10] Although she asked Joseph day after day, he would not go to bed with her.

[11] But one day when Joseph went into the house to do his work, none of the house servants was there. [12] She caught him by his robe and said, "Come to bed with me." But he escaped and ran outside, leaving his robe in her hand. [13] When she saw that he had left his robe and had run out of the house, [14] she called to her house servants and said, "Look at this! This Hebrew that my husband brought to the house is insulting us. He came into my room and tried to rape me, but I screamed as loud as I could. [15] When he heard me scream, he ran outside, leaving his robe beside me."

[16] She kept his robe with her until Joseph's master came home. [17] Then she told him the same story: "That Hebrew slave that you brought here came into my room and insulted me. [18] But when I screamed, he ran outside, leaving his robe beside me."

[19] Joseph's master was furious [20] and had Joseph arrested and put in the prison where the king's prisoners were kept, and there he stayed.

Genesis 39:1-20

Looking Into The Story: In groups of 4, let one person answer question #1. Then, the next person question #2, etc. . . until all four questions are covered. Remember, there are no right or wrong answers.

1. If you were a Hollywood producer and wanted to make a movie around this story, who would you pick to play the role of Joseph?
   a. Arnold Schwarzenegger
   b. Clint Eastwood
   c. Kevin Kostner
   d. Tom Cruise
   e. other:_____

2. Who would you pick to play the part of Potiphar's wife?
   a. Sharon Stone
   b. Whoopi Goldberg
   c. Madonna
   d. Julia Roberts
   e. other:_____

3. Which of the following factors do you think were strongest in Joseph not giving in to Potiphar's wife?
   a. she was probably a real dog
   b. he probably didn't want to get a disease
   c. he was loyal to the man who befriended him
   d. he was gay
   e. he didn't trust her
   f. he knew it was wrong in God's eyes

4. How did Joseph deal with the temptation when Potiphar's wife grabbed him?
   a. he prayed about it
   b. he put his mind on autopilot
   c. he trusted his senses
   d. he got out of there
   e. he tried to reason with her
   f. he had already decided what he was going to do if she grabbed him

5. What does it mean that Joseph ended up in prison because of his moral faithfulness?
   a. it doesn't do any good to do right—people accuse you anyway
   b. that's a female for you—you can't trust them!
   c. what is important is what is right in God's eyes—not people's
   d. Christians should expect to suffer for doing right
   e. other:_____

My Own Story: Note the change in the way you share. Everyone answers question #1 first. Then, go around again on question #2, until you have covered all of the questions.

1. How important is it to you to have a "well built" and "good-looking" body?
   a. I'd kill for such a body!
   b. it's a high priority
   c. if you want to have fun, you've got to look good
   d. it's no big deal, either way
   e. I'd rather not—it just leads to temptation
   f. people with bodies like that are usually shallow

2. Who do you look up to as a role model for someone of your own sex that keeps their body fit?
   a. my parent
   b. a teacher/coach
   c. an athlete I know
   d. a friend
   e. my pastor/youth leader
   f. I don't have anyone

3. Who do you look up to for their physical fitness and spiritual fitness in a healthy balance?
   a. my parent
   b. a teacher/coach
   c. an athlete I know
   d. a friend
   e. my pastor/youth leader

4. Are you more concerned about your physical development or your spiritual development?
   a. physical
   b. spiritual
   c. I keep a balance
   d. I'm not concerned about either

5. What is your greatest motivation to live a clean and holy life?
   a. my love for God—to please him
   b. God's love for me—even though I don't deserve it
   c. my fear of God—not to be punished
   d. my own self respect—to be true to myself
   e. my parents—not to disappoint them
   f. my friends—not to let them down

6. What have you learned that has helped you in dealing with sexual desires?
   a. that sexual desires are normal
   b. that I am not the only one that struggles with sexual desires
   c. that there are healthy ways to deal with sexual desires
   d. that a Christian has been called to refrain from sexual adventures before marriage
   e. that there is forgiveness from God when a Christian asks for it
   f. that my body is the temple of the Holy Spirit

7. What have you found helpful when your date tries to coax you into compromising your Christian principles?

CARING
Teams of 8
15-20 minutes

Getting Personal

Introduction. Here are two options to close the session on problems.

Option 1: Follow the usual procedure. Regather as teams and report in on the session—what you learned—and spend some time in prayer with your prayer partner.

Option 2: Try a new form of sharing prayer requests and praying for one another. If you choose this option, here are the instructions.

1. Get together in groups of three.

2. Let one person share a prayer request by answering the question:

    How can we help you in prayer this week?

3. The other two in the three-some respond to this prayer request in this way:

    • One person prays a prayer of THANKS. . .

    "God, I want to THANK YOU for (name). . . ."

    • The other person prays a prayer of PETITION. . .

    "God, I ask your help for my friend (name), for. . . ."

4. When you have finished with the first person, let the next person share a request and the other two pray for this person, etc. . . around the group of three.

    Remember, in your group of three, you start out by letting one person answer this question:

    How can we help you in prayer this week?

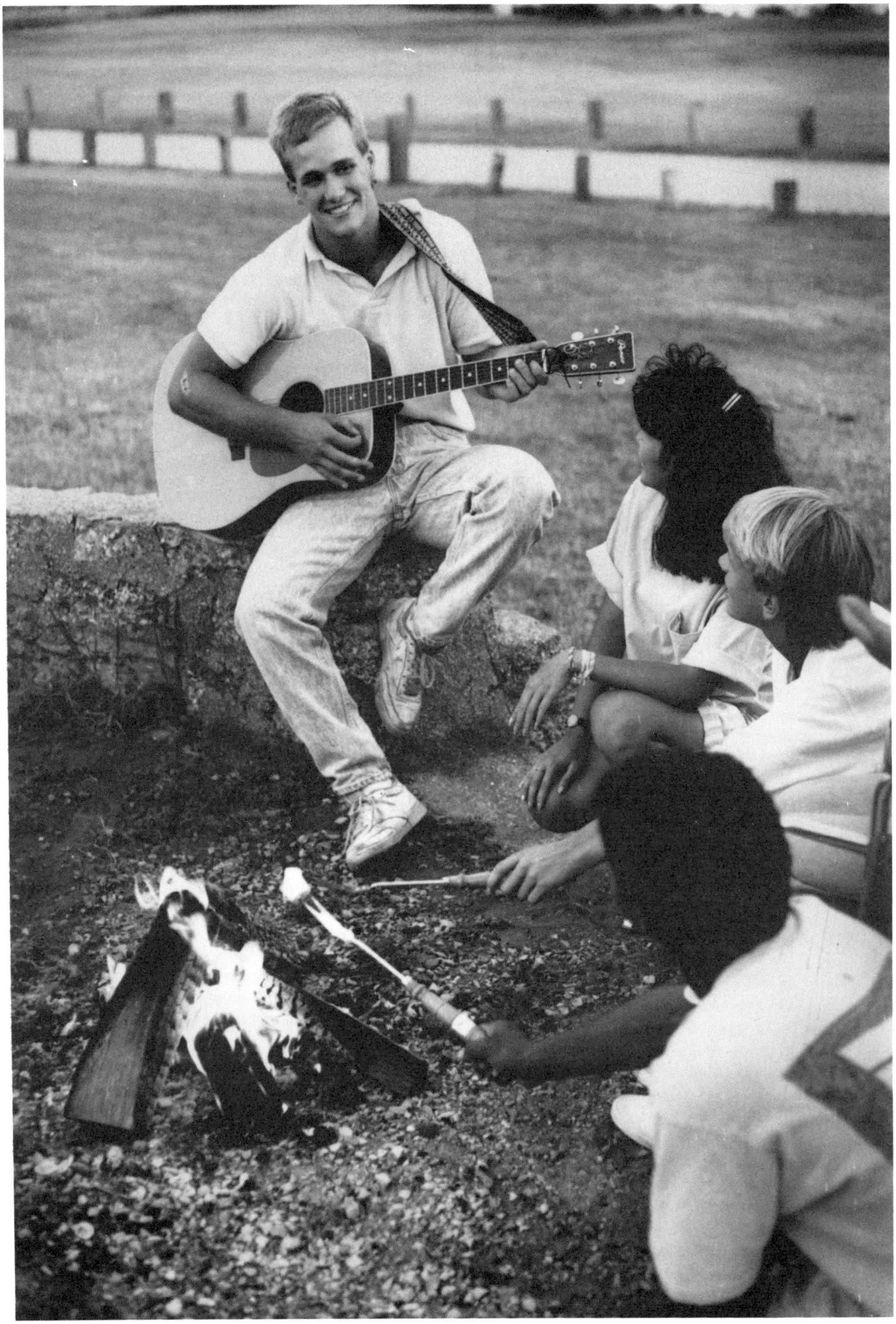

SESSION 6
Spiritual Calling

WARM UP
Groups of 2
15 minutes

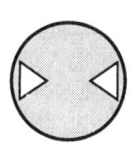

Bumper Stickers

Introduction. Bumper stickers have become a good way for people today to promote something—anything. In a fun way, look over the list below and choose two stickers—one for your front bumper and another for your back bumper. Then, get together with one other person and share. If you have time left over, finish the two sentences below about each other.

___ Soccer is a kick in the grass
___ Danger. Driver spits chewing tobacco
___ Conserve energy—ride a horse
___ Conserve water—shower with a friend
___ Proud parent of an honor student
___ This parent's kid beat up your honor student
___ Outta my way, man
___ My other car is a Mercedes
___ Have you hugged a musician today?
___ Don't bug me—I'm pedaling as fast as I can
___ If you are out of work and hungry, eat an environmentalist
___ I found it
___ Driver in love—stops at all full moons
___ This is not an abandoned car
___ Keep America beautiful—Eat your beer cans
___ One nuclear bomb can ruin your whole day
___ I am the guy your mother warned you about
___ Other:_____

FEEDBACK:

1. Before you explained, I would have guessed that you would probably choose the bumper sticker saying. . .

2. If I could add another bumper sticker to your car that I think would match your personality, I would choose. . .

BIBLE STUDY
Groups of 4
15-30 minutes

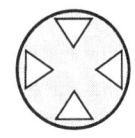

Fishing Episode

Introduction. From now on, the Bible studies in this course will focus on people who make choices in their life—good choices and bad choices. You will be asked to analyze what they did like a "case study." Then, you will be asked to explain what you would do in that situation.

In this session, you will look at a fisherman that Jesus asked to make a choice—a big choice. The discussion questionnaire has multiple-choice options—with no right or wrong answers.

Don't forget to save the last 20-30 minutes for the Caring time at the close. Now listen to the story. Then move into groups of four to discuss the questionnaire.

JESUS CALLS THE FIRST DISCIPLES

¹One day Jesus was standing on the shore of Lake Gennesaret while the people pushed their way up to him to listen to the word of God. ²He saw two boats pulled up on the beach; the fishermen had left them and were washing the nets. ³Jesus got into one of the boats—it belonged to Simon—and asked him to push off a little from the shore. Jesus sat in the boat and taught the crowd.

⁴When he finished speaking, he said to Simon, "Push the boat out further to the deep water, and you and your partners let down your nets for a catch."

⁵"Master," Simon answered, "we worked hard all night long and caught nothing. But if you say so, I will let down the nets." ⁶They let them down and caught such a large number of fish that the nets were about to break. ⁷So they motioned to their partners in the other boat to come and help them. They came and filled both boats so full of fish that the boats were about to sink. ⁸When Simon Peter saw what had happened, he fell on his knees before Jesus and said, "Go away from me, Lord! I am a sinful man!"

⁹He and the others with him were all amazed at the large number of fish they had caught. ¹⁰The same was true of Simon's partners, James and John, the sons of Zebedee. Jesus said to Simon, "Don't be afraid; from now on you will be catching people."

¹¹They pulled the boats up on the beach, left everything, and followed Jesus.   Luke 5:1-11

Looking Into The Story: In groups of 4, let one person answer question #1—choosing one of the options. Then, let the next person answer question #2, etc. . .until you have covered all the questions.

1. What do you think Simon (later called Peter) was thinking when Jesus asked to use his boat to teach in, after Simon had been out fishing all night?
   a. well, as long as you don't assign any homework. . .
   b. why don't you try some <u>real</u> work, buddy?
   c. can you teach me something that will get me a better line of work?
   d. maybe he'll say something that will give me a lift
   e. I'd rather be fishing

2. If you can imagine Peter sitting there in his boat, what was he thinking about while Jesus was teaching the crowd?
   a. oh no—another visiting preacher
   b. his teaching is over my head
   c. I wish he would finish so I can have my boat back
   d. I wish I could go fishing with Jesus
   e. I've always wanted to give my life to something. I wonder if this is it.

3. When do you think Peter made the choice to throw in his life with Jesus?
   a. when he heard Jesus talk to the crowd
   b. when Jesus asked him to go fishing
   c. when they caught "such a large number of fish that their nets were about to break?"
   d. when he tried to get out of it by throwing up his past "sin"
   e. when he left his boat and everything else
   f. years later—after being with Jesus

4. Why did Simon say, "Go away from me, Lord! I am a sinful man!"?
   a. he was afraid Jesus would discover his stash of <u>Playboys</u>
   b. he felt unworthy to be in the presence of such a man
   c. he felt he didn't deserve to have good things happen to him
   d. he wanted to party, and didn't want Jesus around
   e. he was afraid of what Jesus might ask him to do

5. On the day that Peter parked his boat and joined Jesus, what chances would you give this guy of becoming the "rookie" of the year and going on to become an "all star" player on Jesus' team?
   a. a whole lot—he was a promising high school athlete
   b. a little—he was aggressive with lots of nerve
   c. very little—he was second string
   d. none at all—a drop out

My Own Story: In groups of 4, everyone answer question #1 first. Then, go around again on question #2, etc.

1. When was the first time you recall feeling the tug of Jesus on your heart?
   a. when I was very young
   b. when there was a crisis in my life
   c. when I was away on a retreat
   d. just recently
   e. I don't know that I have

2. How are you and Jesus getting along now?
   a. we're not talking
   b. we're dating a little
   c. we're going steady
   d. we're arguing lately
   e. we have broken up
   f. Jesus who?

3. If Jesus invited you to "push out into the deep water", what would you say?
   a. I'm not into deep water fishing
   b. I'm afraid of the deep water
   c. I'll have to check with my friends first
   d. fine, as long as I can stand on the shore
   e. great, let's go for it
   f. other:_____

4. What if you could get your entire youth group to join you in some "deep water" fishing, would you be interested?
   a. sure, but I don't think everybody is willing
   b. well, I'll think about it
   c. I'll have to check with my mother
   d. I'm not the adventurous type as you know
   e. great, when do we start
   f. what is "deep water fishing"?

5. How would you finish this sentence? I am committed to know and follow the will of God for my life. . .
   a. all of the time
   b. most of the time
   c. some of the time
   d. on occasion

6. What would it mean for you "to be catching people" for Jesus?
   a. to witness to my friends
   b. to be inviting friends to church
   c. to show people God's love through my love
   d. to start focusing on people rather than things

7. In order to "catch people" for Jesus, what do you have going for you that is "good bait" (good to help draw people to Jesus)?
   a. my ability to make friends
   b. my ability to listen when people have problems
   c. my knowledge of the Bible
   d. my willingness to risk
   e. my willingness to "walk my talk"
   f. my willingness to help people in need
   g. my openness to people of different cultures
   h. other:_____

CARING
Teams of 8
15-20 minutes

Learning to Care

Introduction: You are nearly through with this course as a youth group. Next week, you will have a chance to celebrate and decide what you are going to do next.

To prepare for your last session together, take a few minutes right now and reflect on what and where you have changed during this course. If you have stayed with the same team throughout this course, you will be able to say how you have seen your teammates change. If you don't know each other that well, you will do the talking for yourself. Here are two steps to follow.

1. **Affirmation.** Go around and let everyone on your team answer one or more of the questions below. Again, if you know each other, use this opportunity to share how you have seen your teammates grow.

    - Where have you grown in your own life during this course?
    - Where have you seen growth in some of the others in your group during this course?
    - What have you appreciated most about the group during this course?

2. **Option.** At this point, your team can choose one of two ways to close the meeting.

    - **Option 1: Prayer Partners.** Get together with your prayer partner and report on your week. Then close in prayer.

    - **Option 2: Circle of Love.** Stay together with your team and express your feelings for each other non-verbally. Here is how. Follow carefully:

        a. Stand in a circle—about a foot apart
        b. Everyone puts their right hand in front of them—palm up
        c. Team leader steps into the circle and goes to one person. Looks them in the eyes for a few seconds. Then, takes their hand and tries to express the care you feel for this person by doing something to their hand—such as gripping it firmly, stroking it, shaking it...etc. Use only appropriate gestures.
        d. After the Team Leader has gone around the circle, the next person goes around the circle in the same way, etc... until everyone has gone around the circle.

    Remember, all of this is done <u>without words.</u>

    BUT IN SHAKING THE HANDS OF THOSE IN YOUR GROUP, YOU CAN SAY A LOT—HOW YOU CARE!

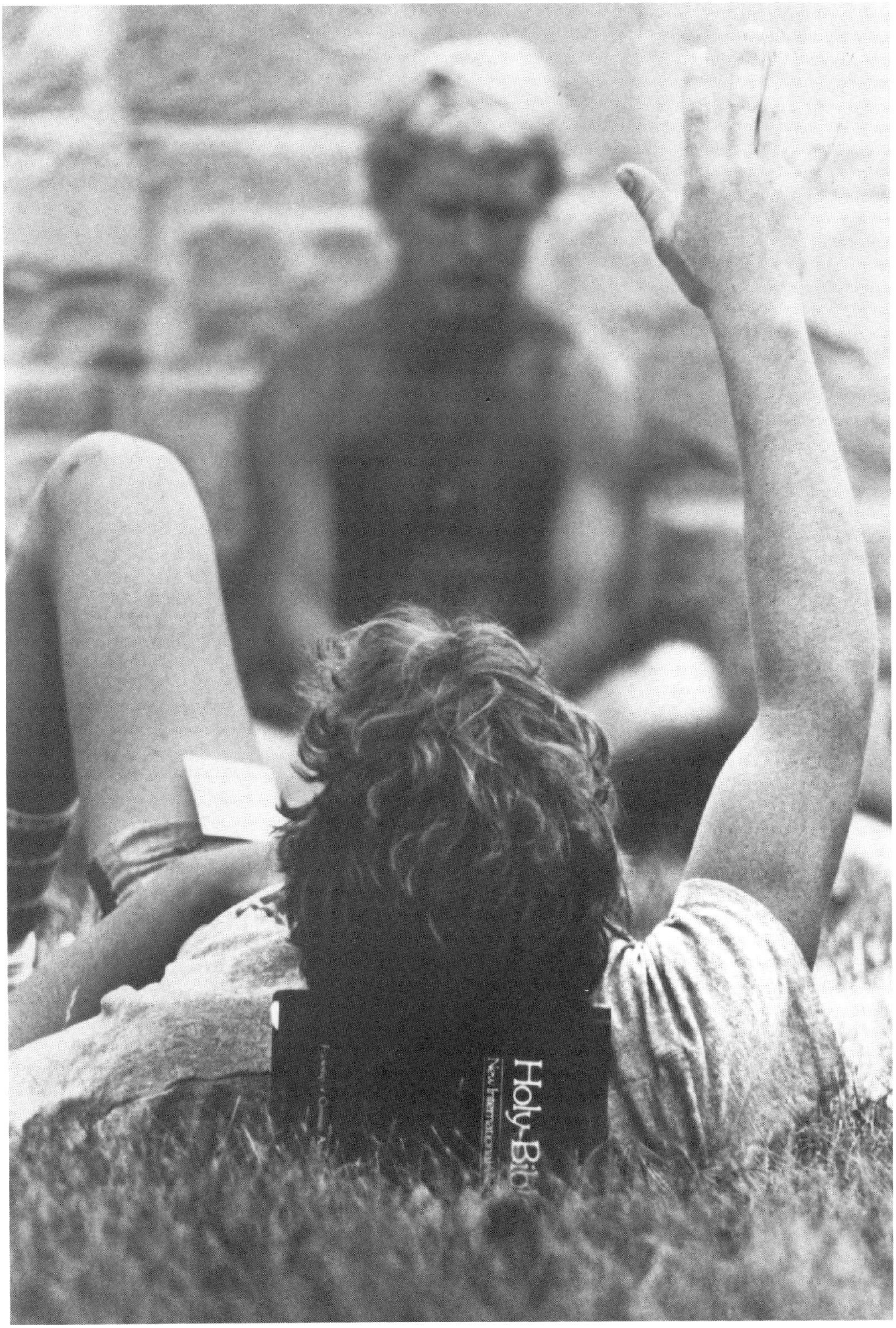

SESSION 7
Bottom Line

WARM UP
Groups of 2
15 minutes

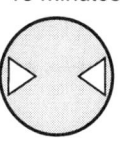

Broadway Jobs

Introduction. In this last session, take some time to share a word of appreciation for your teammates—how they helped make this course special for you. You need to know people to be able to do this Warm Up activity.

Now, in silence read over the list of workers that are needed to put on a Broadway show. Place one person's name on the blank that best exemplifies that particular job. Devote a few minutes right now to do this exercise which will be shared at the close of this session at the beginning of the Caring Time. You can use their name only once and you have to use everyone's name once—so think it through before you jot down their names.

Remember, you share these later.

____ PRODUCER: Typical Hollywood business tycoon; extravagant, big-budget, big-production magnate in the David O. Selznik style.

____ DIRECTOR: Creative, imaginative brains behind the scene; perfectionist, big-spender, unpredictable genius.

____ HEROINE: Beautiful, captivating, seductive, everybody's heart throb, defenseless when men are around, but nobody's fool.

____ HERO: Tough, macho, champion of the underdog, knight in shining armor, Mr. Clutch in the John Wayne mold, always gets his man.

____ COMEDIAN: Childlike, happy-go-lucky, outrageously funny, covers up a brilliant interior with the carefully tailored "dim" exterior.

____ CHARACTER PERSON: One-of-a-kind eccentric, rugged individualist, outrageously different, colorful, adds spice to any surrounding.

____ FALL GUY: Studied, nonchalant character, who wins the hearts of everyone by being the "foil" of the heavy characters.

____ TECHNICAL DIRECTOR: The genius for "sound and lights," complete with beard, tennis shoes, "off the wall" T-shirt and jogging shorts.

More on Next Page

____ COMPOSER OF LYRICS: Communicates in music what everybody understands, heavy into feelings, moods, outbursts of energy.

____ PUBLICITY AGENT: Mafia leader turned Madison Avenue executive, knows all the angles, good at one-liners, a flair for "hot" news.

____ VILLAIN: The "bad guy" who really is the heavy for the plot, forces others to think, challenges traditional values; out to destroy "cliches," shallow morality, and plastic conformity.

____ AUTHOR: Shy, aloof, eccentric person, very much in touch with feelings, sensitive to people, puts into words what others only feel.

____ STAGEHAND: Supportive, behind-the-scenes person who makes things run smoothly; patient, subtle, unflappable.

BIBLE STUDY
Groups of 4
15-30 minutes

A Solid Foundation

Introduction. The Bible study for this session is about two kinds of house builders. Jesus used this parable at the close of the Sermon on the Mount to illustrate two kinds of people. And it would be fitting at the close of this course on CHOICES to use this graphic illustration. Listen to the story carefully, then move into groups of four and discuss the questionnaire. Be sure to save enough time at the close to evaluate this course as a youth group and to decide what you are going to do next. If you are planning a special service or celebration at the close, you may have to cut this Bible study short.

[24]"So then, anyone who hears these words of mine and obeys them is like a wise man who built his house on rock. [25]The rain poured down, the rivers flooded over, and the wind blew hard against that house. But it did not fall, because it was built on rock. [26]"But anyone who hears these words of mine and does not obey them is like a foolish man who built his house on sand. [27]The rain poured down, the rivers flooded over, the wind blew hard against that house, and it fell. And what a terrible fall that was!"
Matthew 7:24-27

Looking Into The Story: In groups of 4, let one person answer question #1, the next person answer question #2, etc. There are no right or wrong answers.

1. Why do you think the one guy decided to build his house on sand?
    a. he wanted a beach in his backyard
    b. it was an easier place to dig
    c. his parents told him not to, so he had no other choice
    d. he could get the land at a bargain price

2. Whose fault was it—that the houses built on the sand collapsed?
    a. nobody's fault—it was the bad weather that caused it
    b. the builder's fault—for building on the sand
    c. the government's—for letting the builder build where he did

3. If you were the bank, would you give the owner of the house that collapsed another loan to build again?
   a. sure, he learned his lesson
   b. maybe, if he cried and begged and promised to build better next time
   c. no, not unless he showed me the rock he was going to build the foundation on

4. What exactly is Jesus promising to someone who is willing to live by his words?
   a. that you will never have stormy weather
   b. that you will have the same stormy weather as everybody else
   c. that the stormy weather will not undermine your life
   d. that you will get a new house if the old one collapses

My Own Story: In groups of 4, take this inventory on your spiritual life together. The first part is the inventory. The second part is the reflection.

PERSONAL INVENTORY

Part 1: If you could compare your life to a house, and every room in your house to a living space in your life, what would a building inspector say?

Let one person in your group read the description of one room below. Then, let everyone in your group call out a number from 1 to 10—1 being SHAKY and 10 being EXCELLENT. Then, go on to the next room and let everyone call out a number for this room.

Remember, you are a building inspector. The number you call out indicates the grade you give on this room in your life.

LIVING ROOM: I have my life in order. I know what I want to do; my values are well defined; my moral principles are clear; I am feeling good about myself and my lifestyle right now.

   1   2   3   4   5   6   7   8   9   10

RECREATION ROOM: I have a healthy balance in my schedule for leisure; I use my spare time carefully—to restore my mind and spirit as well as my body. I am feeling good about my priorities and the way I use my time.

   1   2   3   4   5   6   7   8   9   10

FAMILY ROOM: I have a good relationship with my parents and brothers and sisters. We have learned to talk about our differences; we deal with our conflicts; we "build up" one another when "outside weather" is a problem; I am feeling good about my family and enjoy being with them.

   1   2   3   4   5   6   7   8   9   10

LIBRARY ROOM: I have a balanced diet in my learning habits for mental and spiritual stimulation as well as pleasure. I try to think for myself, to make my own decisions based on definite values and moral principles, and don't just "cave in" to the pressure of my friends.

1   2   3   4   5   6   7   8   9   10

PHYSICAL FITNESS ROOM: I try to keep in shape: to deal with flabbiness. I feel good about my manhood/womanhood and sexuality, but I do not let my sexual desires get the best of me. I can sleep nights and weather the "storms" without getting fatigued and depressed.

1   2   3   4   5   6   7   8   9   10

GUEST ROOM: I have a good relationship with my friends and schoolmates. I enjoy being with people without feeling dependent upon them. I can belong to the crowd without accepting or bowing to their values. I can stand against social pressure to conform, yet am sensitive to open the door when someone needs a little warmth.

1   2   3   4   5   6   7   8   9   10

REFLECTION

Part 2: Go around on the first question and let everyone answer. Then, go around again on question #2, etc. Remember to save the last 30 minutes for the Caring time.

1. If you could compare your spiritual foundation right now to a house, what would it be?
   a. shaky
   b. firm
   c. brand new
   d. temporary
   e. better
   f. slipping

2. Where have you seen the most progress in your life recently?
   a. in my self confidence
   b. in developing my athletic abilities
   c. in dealing with relationships
   d. in sorting out my priorities
   e. in knowing what I believe
   f. in taking a stand on things—like moral issues
   g. in my school work
   h. other:_____

CARING
Teams of 8
15-20 minutes

What Happened?

Introduction: You have two options for this special closing experience: (1) A de-briefing session, using the agenda below, or (2) The worship service as described in the Coach's Book, Session 7, of the book Choices.

1. **Warm Up Exercise:** Regather as teams (or the entire youth group together) and share the results of the Warm Up exercise. Ask one person to sit in silence while everyone on their team explains where they have put this person's name and why. Then, move to the next person, etc. around the group. Use this opportunity to share your appreciation for the contributions you have made to each other on the team.

2. **Evaluation:** Go around on the first question below and let everyone explain their answer. Then, go around again on the next question, etc.

    A. When you first started on this course, what did you think about it?
      a. I liked it
      b. I had some reservations
      c. I only came for the fun
      d. I was bored
      e. other:_____

    B. How would you describe the experience of opening up and sharing your ideas and problems with this group?
      a. scary
      b. very difficult
      c. exciting
      d. a life-changing experience
      e. invaluable
      f. okay, but. . .
      g. just what I needed
      h. a beautiful breakthrough

    C. What was the high point in this program for you?
      a. fun
      b. times of prayer
      c. feeling of belonging to others who really care
      d. being with teammates who are committed to Christ
      e. knowing I am not alone in my problems
      f. finding myself again
      g. Bible study
      h. learning to deal with my hang-ups

3. **Personal Change.** Turn back to page 3 and let everyone explain where they have changed during this course.

4. **What's Next.** As a group, decide what you are going to do next.

A Word To The Youth Leaders

Congratulations. You are working with the most potential-packed audience in the world—Teenagers. This is one of the most difficult times in their lives. They are making big decisions, often alone or in packs. Peers are important to them and there is tremendous pressure to do what peers demand and the chance to think critically about choices. This youth program is designed to give teenagers a feeling of belonging. A family of peers. An alternative to the gang at school. Or an alternative inside of the school.

This program is built around the idea of teamwork. The goal is to help youth "bring out the best in one another." By agreeing on a set of goals. Agreeing on a level of commitment for a period of time (seven weeks). By setting ground rules, and holding each other accountable. If this sounds like something out of educational psychology, it is. The dynamics are the same. The only difference is the motive and the learning objective. The goal of this program is spiritual formation. Christian orientation. Christian value clarification. Christian moral development. Christian commitment.

The Importance Of Voluntary Commitment

The difference between this program and the typical youth program in the church is the commitment level. To get into this program, a youth *must* commit himself or herself to being in the program. This means "choosing" to be in the program every session for seven weeks, to be a team player in order to make the group process work.

Anyone who has been involved in team sports will understand this principle. And anyone who has coached a team will understand the role of the student pastor or youth leader. The youth leader is the coach and the youth group is the squad. And the squad is broken up into small units or teams of six to eight—with a sub-coach or facilitator inside of each team.

Structure Of The Youth Meetings

The meetings look like typical training workouts of a sports camp. First, the whole squad meets together for some limbering up exercises (all together or by teams of eight competing against one another if you have a large youth group). Then, the entire squad pairs off for some basic, one-on-one "conversation starters" to break the ice. Then, with your partner, groups of four are formed for the Bible Study discussion. Finally, the team of eight is regathered for a little wrap-up and caring for each other. The typical meeting looks like this:

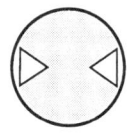

Step 1:	Step 2:	Step 3:	Step 4:
Crowd Breaker	Conversation	Bible Study/	Wrap Up and
Team of 8	Starters/	Groups of 4	Caring/
or all together	Groups of 2	or half of team	Teams of 8

Moving from the large group (Step 1) to groups of two (Step 2) to groups of 4 (Step 3) to groups of 8 (Step 4) will not only offer a spontaneity to the meeting, but will also position the youth to be in the best size of group for the particular type of activity.

Step 1:	**Step 2:**	**Step 3:**	**Step 4:**
Purpose: To Kick off the meeting.	Purpose: To start a relationship	Purpose: To discuss Bible Story	Purpose: To care for one another.

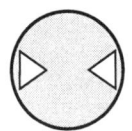

In the first session in this course, the ideal would be to form teams of eight that can stay together for the entire course. This could be done by random selection or by designating the teams to break up cliques. Or it can be done in a serendipitous fashion by giving out slips of song titles and having the youth find out who is on their team by whistling their song until they "find each other." For junior highs, we recommend that an adult or older youth be in each team of eight.

If you only have fifteen or twenty youth in your entire group, you could keep all of the squad together for Step 1 and Step 4, and break into 2's and 4's for Step 2 and Step 3.

In Case of Emergency, Read the Instructions

In the margin beside each Step, you will find instructions to the leader. Read this. Sometimes, the instructions are important. Trust us. We have written this program based on our experience. Give the program a chance. There is method to the madness. Particularly, the fast-paced movement from 2's to 4's to 8's.

Get a commitment out of your youth before you start the program for seven weeks or seven sessions. And remind them (by thanking them every week) for making this commitment. Here's to the thing that God is about to do in your youth. Here's to the future of your church—your youth.

Serendipity House is a publisher specializing in small groups. Serendipity has been providing training and resources for youth ministry for over 30 years. As we continue to develop materials for youth groups, we would love to hear your comments, ideas or suggestions. Call us at 1-800-525-9563.

SERENDIPITY HOUSE

SERENDIPITY HOUSE is a publishing house that creates programs like this one for many types of groups in the church: kick off groups, Bible study groups, support groups, recovery groups and mission/task groups. The philosophy behind these groups is the same: (1) help the group agree upon their purpose and ground rules, (2) spend the first few sessions you are together getting acquainted, (3) shift gears in Bible study as the group matures, and (4) help the group say "goodbye" and decompress when they are through with their purpose.

ABOUT LYMAN COLEMAN THE AUTHOR

LYMAN COLEMAN has been training youth leaders in the Serendipity method for group building for many, many years (more than he wants to remember).

While in graduate school (New York University), he studied the coffee house experiments and created a model for church-sponsored coffee houses with the youth group serving as the support team. He helped design the group-based program for huddle groups for the Fellowship of Christian Athletes, Marriage Encounter and Faith At Work, combining Scripture study with values clarification, moral development and educational psychology.

This series of youth Bible study courses was originally co-written with Denny Rydberg, President of Young Life. The uniqueness of this series of Bible studies is the group approach to Scripture study—where group building is central in the sharing and caring for one another in a group.

Hundreds of youth workers have contributed their ideas and dozens of youth leaders have had a part in writing these studies, including David Stone, Don Kimball, Richard Peace, Keith Madsen and the entire Serendipity staff.